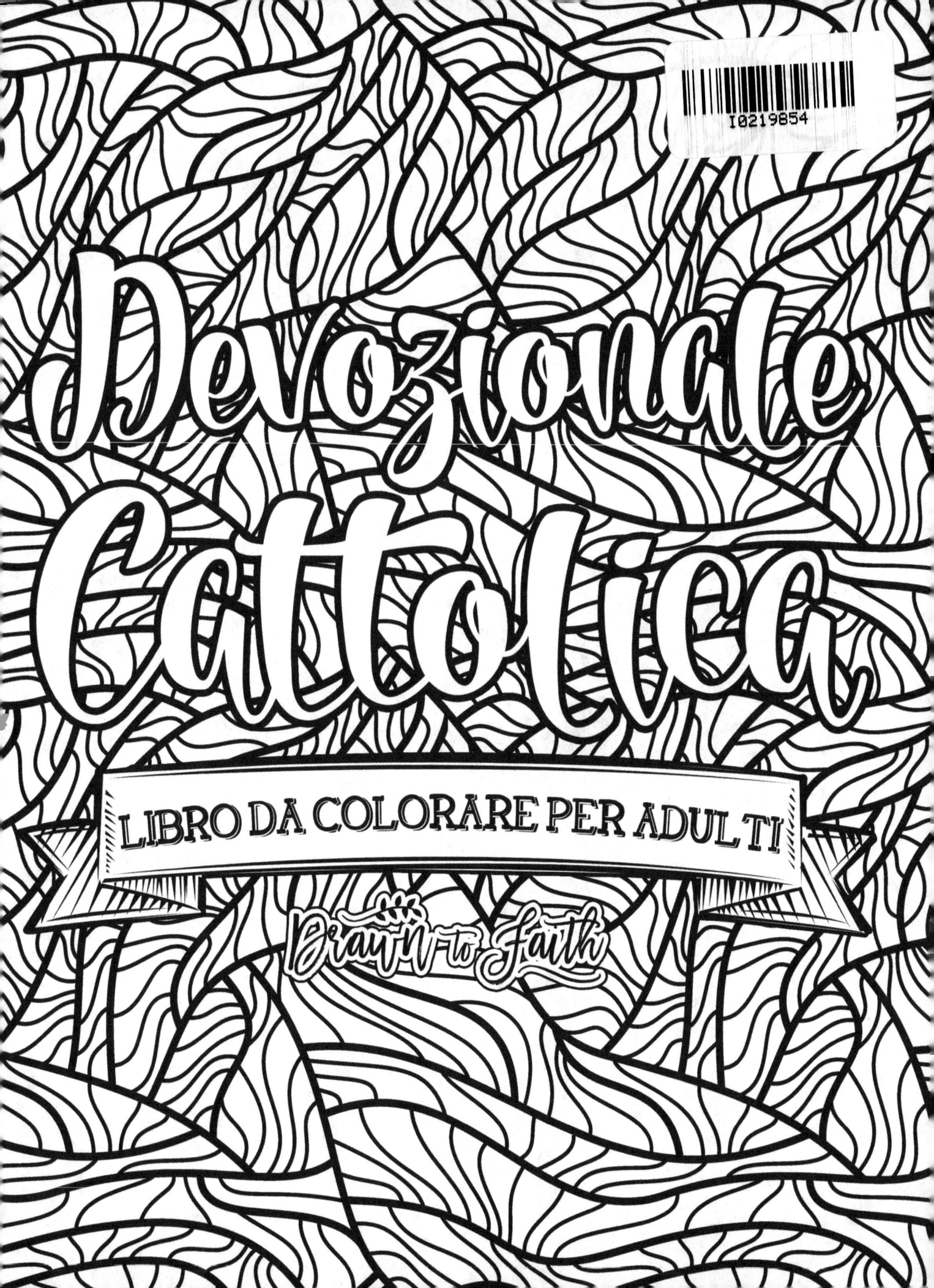

Copyright © 2016 Drawn to Faith

Scripture texts in this work are taken from the New American Bible, revised edition © 2010, 1991, 1986, 1970 Confraternity of Christian Doctrine, Washington, D.C. and are used by permission of the copyright owner. All Rights Reserved. No part of the New American Bible may be reproduced in any form without permission in writing from the copyright owner.

All rights reserved.

ISBN-13: 978-1-945888-79-3
ISBN-10: 1-945888-79-2

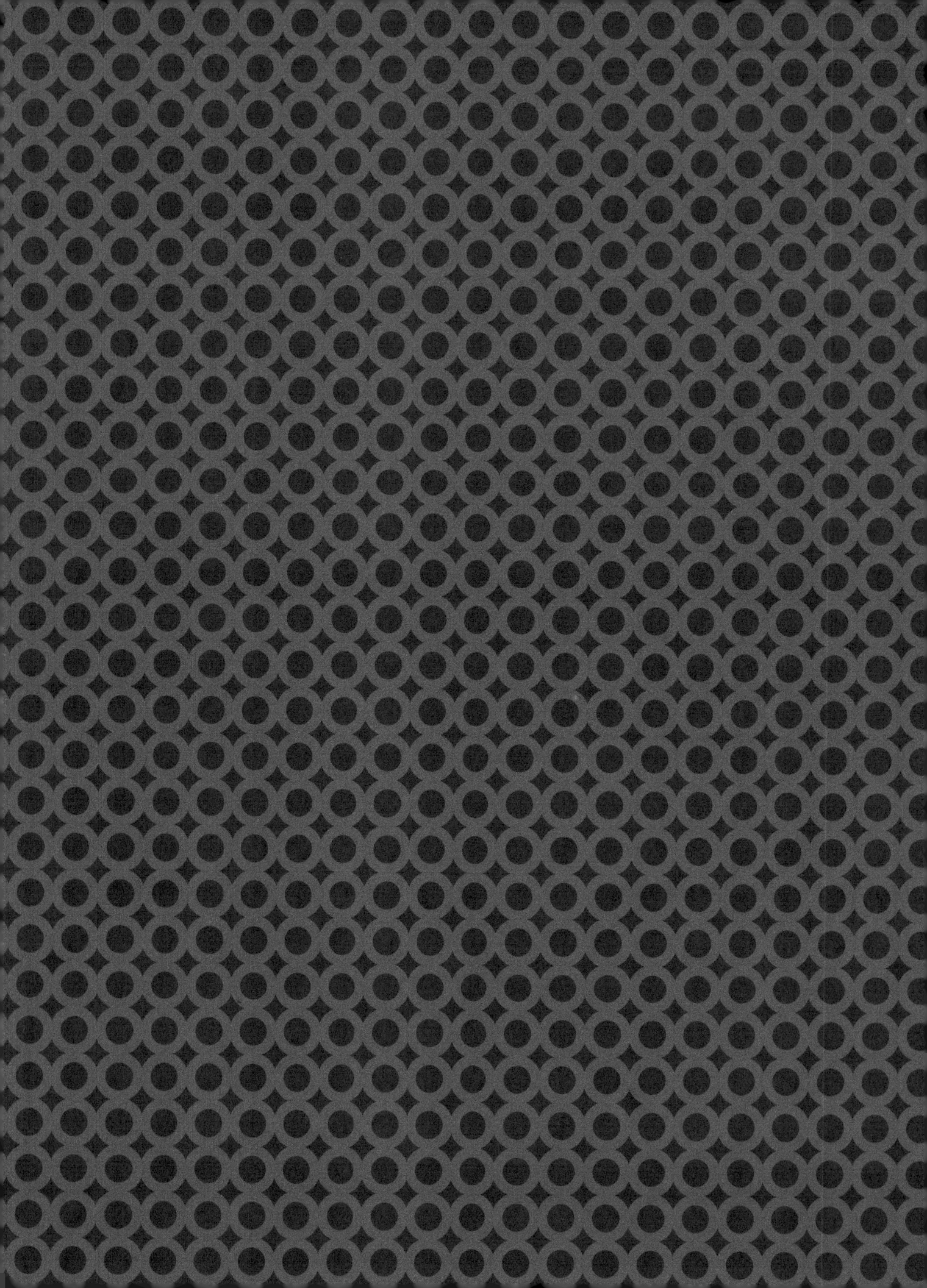

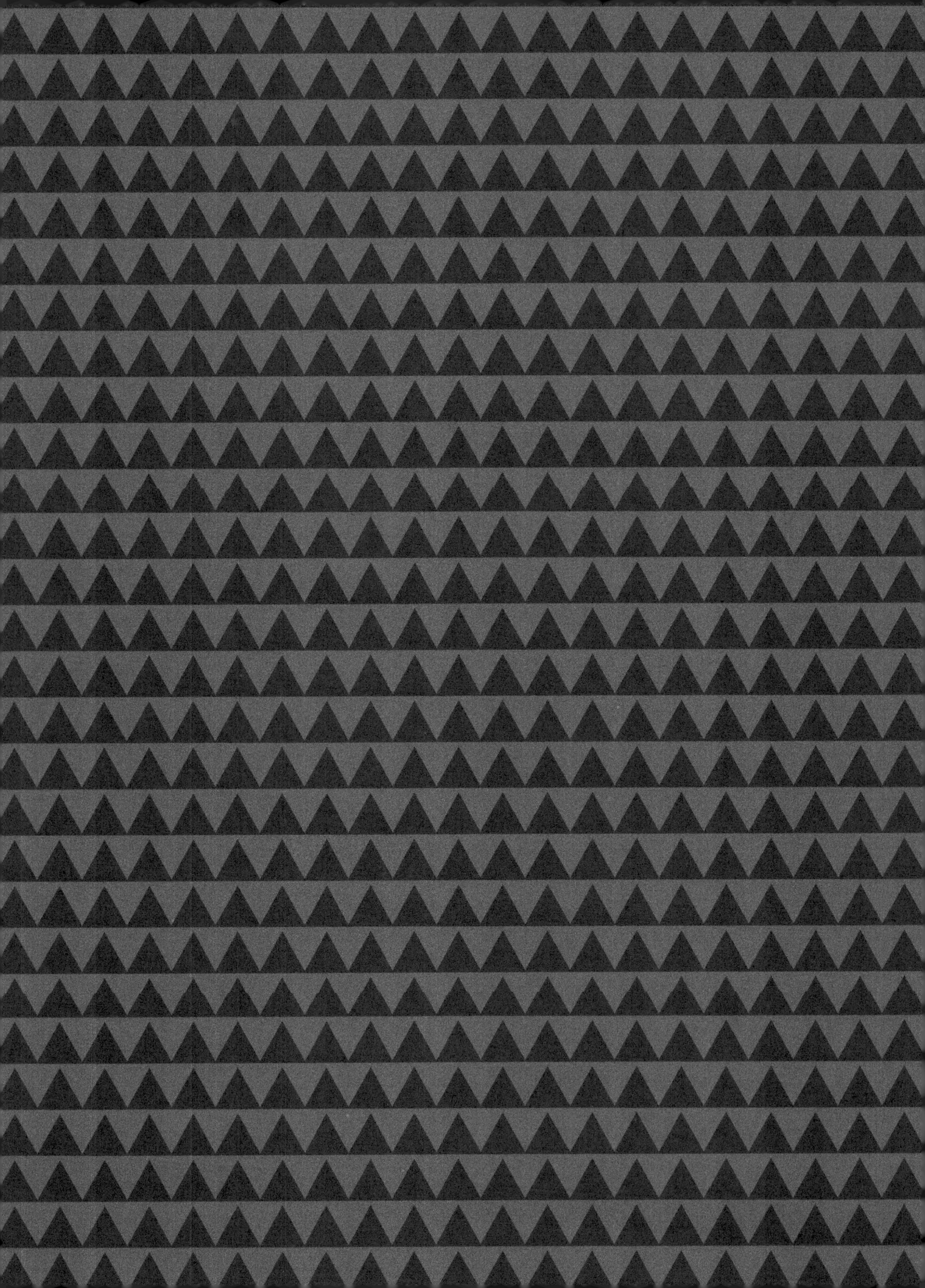

BE SURE TO FOLLOW US ON SOCIAL MEDIA FOR THE LATEST NEWS, SNEAK PEEKS, & GIVEAWAYS

@drawntofaith

Drawn To Faith

@drawntofaith

ADD YOURSELF TO OUR MONTHLY NEWSLETTER FOR FREE DIGITAL DOWNLOADS AND DISCOUNT CODES

www.drawntofaith.com/newsletter

CHECK OUT OUR OTHER BOOKS!

www.drawntofaith.com

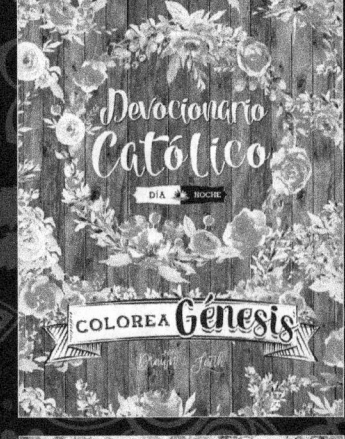

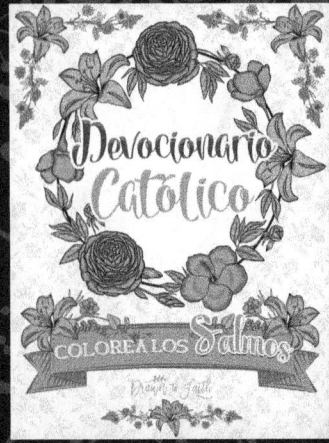
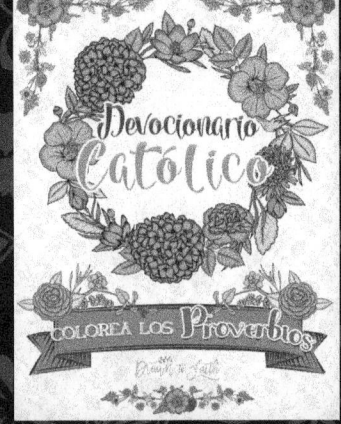
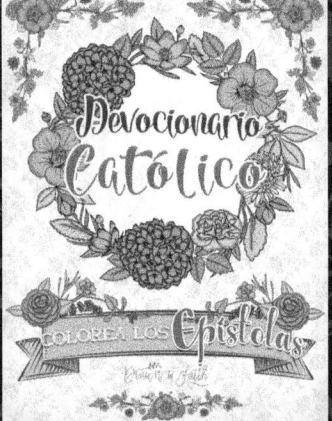